THE LITTLE BOOK OF GENIUS

The Little Book of Genius

Miracles

Adam C. Hall, Alan Cohen, Debra Landwehr Engle

Waterside Productions

Copyright © 2023 by Adam C. Hall, Alan Cohen, and Debra Engle

All rights reserved. This book or any portion thereof may not be reproduced or used in any manner whatsoever without the express written permission of the publisher except for the use of brief quotations in articles and book reviews.

ISBN-13: 978-1-958848-60-9 hardcover edition
ISBN-13: 978-1-958848-61-6 paperback edition
ISBN-13: 978-1-958848-62-3 e-book edition

Waterside Productions
2055 Oxford Ave
Cardiff, CA 92007
www.waterside.com

TABLE OF CONTENTS

Foreword · vii
Introduction · ix

Wisdom Teaching 1: True Forgiveness · · · · · · · · · · · · · · 1
Wisdom Teaching 2: True Purpose · · · · · · · · · · · · · · · 7
Wisdom Teaching 3: Death · · · · · · · · · · · · · · · · · · · 11
Wisdom Teaching 4: Divine Life · · · · · · · · · · · · · · · · 15
Wisdom Teaching 5: Peace · · · · · · · · · · · · · · · · · · · 19
Wisdom Teaching 6: Love · 23
Wisdom Teaching 7: True Function · · · · · · · · · · · · · · 27
Wisdom Teaching 8: Destiny · · · · · · · · · · · · · · · · · · 33
Wisdom Teaching 9: Divine Doing · · · · · · · · · · · · · · · 37
Wisdom Teaching 10: Divine Being · · · · · · · · · · · · · · · 41
Wisdom Teaching 11: Divine Evolution · · · · · · · · · · · · 47
Wisdom Teaching 12: Divine Involution · · · · · · · · · · · · 51
Wisdom Teaching 13: Unification · · · · · · · · · · · · · · · · 55

About the Authors · 61

Foreword

Integrating my spiritual life with my physical journey has been an ongoing education for me. While I am at times tempted to believe that there are certain rules I need to master to be successful in the world, and others that apply to the spiritual dimension, I am learning that my earthly life is an extension of spiritual reality.

While this book is titled *The Little Book of Genius*, there is nothing little about genius. God has imbued all of us with His own brilliant mind, and when we learn to think with God, we find all we need to know to live a happy, healthy, productive life.

My contributions to this book, alongside stories from Adam and Debra, catalog my experiences in achieving the mystical marriage of divinity and humanity, the sacred and the social. It is my sincere prayer that these stories and ideas touch you at the level of soul and help you claim the magnificent spiritual adventure that your earthly journey is intended to be.

—Alan Cohen

INTRODUCTION

Welcome to *The Little Book of Genius: MIRACLES*. Within it, you'll discover the power of your mind to create everyday miracles—shifts in your thinking from fear to love.

At the core of each volume in *The Little Book of Genius Series* are 13 Wisdom Teachings, which were communicated through an enlightened spirit guide. The teachings lead us through the principles of living a life of deep inner joy—the greatest hallmark of success.

Bringing the teachings to *The Little Book of Genius Series* has been an act of wholeness and intention. Our lives seem to be built on the smallest, most everyday decisions and choices. Yet every decision is a choice to believe that you can be limited by the demands of the world around you and your own ego mind—or grow and extend love.

Our desire is to bring the 13 Wisdom Teachings to you in ways that are practical, relevant, and simple to apply. That's why every volume includes stories, practical steps, and occasional mantras to help you incorporate the teachings into your busy life.

Many of the teachings in this particular volume are based on *A Course in Miracles*, a program of spiritual psychotherapy that has transformed lives around the world. That program has at its core this simple but profound teaching:

"See only love, for that is what you are."

The word *love* is synonymous with peace, contentment, joy, abundance, well-being, generosity, gratitude—every expression of the Divine energy that created you. In our physical human selves, we have ego minds that dwell in the deep fear of not being enough. But our higher Self knows that we are more than our small egos. We are extensions of Source. When we learn to think with that Mind of God, we experience and share miracles in this world. We begin to see through the lens of love not because of what we're looking upon, but because of the eyes we're seeing through.

This *Little Book of Genius* offers 13 Wisdom Teachings—universal principles that will lead you to the clarity of your own Genius Mind, liberating you from feelings of scarcity, struggle, and sacrifice.

Within each Wisdom Teaching, you'll find a story and insights that are as simple as one, two, three. You may recognize yourself or your thought patterns in many of the teachings. And you'll see how the principles enable you to move from old patterns of blame, shame, guilt, sadness, anger, and stress to a new life rich with inner blessings.

If you feel triggered about something during your day, simply open this *Little Book* to any page and receive the insights that will help you move past life's most challenging moments.

Carry this book with you. Tuck it inside your purse or backpack. Read it over and over and practice the teachings with joy and gratitude. Every time you do, you'll open up new channels of understanding within you.

And you'll be an even more conscious creator from your Genius Mind, manifesting the miracles of inner peace you so richly deserve.

With blessings,
Adam C. Hall and Debra Engle

Our Contributor

In this volume of *The Little Book of Genius*, we're honored and grateful to include the work of Alan Cohen, a master spiritual teacher and author of thirty books. You'll find Alan's stories in the Wisdom Teachings on True Forgiveness, True Purpose, Love, True Function, Divine Being, and Unification.

WISDOM TEACHING 1
TRUE FORGIVENESS

True Forgiveness

> God's Will for me is perfect happiness.
> There is no sin; it has no consequence.
> —*A Course in Miracles*

The world's idea of forgiveness is, "You did something really bad that hurt me, but I will overlook it." Spirit's idea of forgiveness is, "Nothing you do can take away my peace. I claim power over my happiness, and I release you from the mistaken notion that you are in charge of my happiness."

While I was visiting Spokane, Washington, my friend Alden, a dedicated *A Course in Miracles* (*ACIM*) student, offered to drive me wherever I needed to go. We made an appointment for him to pick me up one afternoon at a certain spot and take me to my next engagement.

Just before our meeting, I had a massage, and I fell asleep on the massage table. The compassionate therapist let me sleep after the session. When I woke up, I realized I had missed my meeting time with Alden. I felt terribly guilty. Here this kind fellow had devoted his precious time to help me, and I stood him up with a self-indulgent massage.

When I saw Alden the next day, I apologized profusely. "I'm so sorry I missed your ride," I told him as I explained what had happened.

Alden smiled and replied, "No problem. Would you like a ride anywhere today?"

I was stunned. Many people would have taken the attitude, "You blew off our meeting. Why should I do something nice for you now?"

But Alden, an *ACIM* teacher of love, decided to put the Course maxim into practice: demonstrate to your brother that his perceived "sin"—simply an error in thinking—has had no effect.

1. True forgiveness teaches that the "sin" the other person believes he or she has committed has not marred the reality of love. "Sin," in the mind of the world, creates an unredeemable loss. When you demonstrate that another person's (or your own) sin has not caused a loss, you wipe out the belief and the perceived cost of sin in their mind (or yours), and you free both of you from the karma that the world teaches is so solid and unforgivable.
2. When you free another, you free yourself. When you hold a judgment, you are keeping another person in a kind of psychic jail. Meanwhile, you have to sit at the door of their cell to make sure they don't escape, so you are in jail with them. Their imprisonment is your own, and freeing them is a gift to yourself.
3. There is a difference between a sin and an error. Sin requires punishment, but an error simply requires correction. We have all made plenty of errors, but we have never sinned. The word *sin* comes from ancient Hebrew and Greek languages, meaning "to miss the

mark." In archery, when you miss the bullseye, you don't fall on the ground, flail, beat your chest, and ask what your punishment or penance will be. That would be an utter waste of time. The only reasonable response is to learn from your error, take another shot, and strive to do better. The Course tells us that guilt is never justified. Correction, on the other hand, is a mature, doable path of learning.

Wisdom Teaching 2
True Purpose

True Purpose

> The purpose of life is a life of purpose.
> —Robert Byrne

While we have been taught that we have many purposes, such as being a wife, a teacher, a Christian, a programmer, or a yogi, our deeper purpose is to make every moment count no matter our outer role. Ultimately our only real purpose is to know ourselves as God created us and live from that divine identity.

As a teenager, Steven Spielberg took a tour of Universal Studios. During a bathroom break, he hid in a stall and then slipped out to explore the movie lot. He struck up a friendship with the studio librarian, who gave him a three-day pass to visit the studio.

By the end of those three days, the studio guards got to know him, so they just waved him past the gate. Spielberg found an empty office, put his name on the office directory, dressed the part of an executive, and learned a great deal about how the studio operated. This ruse went on for two-and-a-half months until he had to go back to school.

When Spielberg later completed his first 35 mm film, *Amblin'*, he showed it to producers at Universal, and they offered him a deal. The rest is, of course, history. Steven Spielberg went on to become the most famous, respected, and successful movie director and producer in motion picture history.

1. In addition to our spiritual purpose to know ourselves as divine beings, we have a purpose in the world. As we recognize and follow that purpose, we become all that we were born to be, and we enjoy the deep soul satisfaction of living our true callings. Some people deny the world as separate from God. Yet the world can be a powerful venue in which God delivers gifts and blessings to humanity through people.
2. Following your true purpose may call you to step outside the world's rules and expectations for you. Spielberg broke the rules of the tour and the studio, but he went on to become the best thing that ever happened to Universal Studios. *A Course in Miracles* asks us to remember, "I am under no laws but God's."
3. When you follow your purpose, you are in the best position to help others follow theirs. Spielberg has brought entertainment, delight, and profound spiritual messages to billions of people, uplifting their lives. Likewise, when you are true to your unique calling, Spirit will send all the right people to you for their healing and upliftment, and yours.

WISDOM TEACHING 3
DEATH

DEATH

> There is no death, but there *is* a belief in death.
> —*A Course in Miracles*

You've probably seen a T-shirt with a saying something like this: "Shit happens, and then we die."

That perfectly captures the ego's belief, which can be summarized this way: "We live in bodies that are at constant risk of being hurt, we do our best to struggle our way through life and make people love us, and in the end, when it's over, it's over. We don't deserve any more than that." No wonder we have epidemics of loneliness and despair.

Our higher selves, on the other hand, know the truth. We are eternal spirits or souls, born into bodies to experience adventures in a world of contrasts. Those contrasts, properly perceived, cause us to expand and extend more love. Eventually our bodies will cease to exist, but our spirits will live on to continue creating and growing. Everything we experience contributes to love and an expansion of light in the universe.

This shift in our thinking about death changes our entire orientation to life.

1. Our egos spend much of their time trying to stay alive. In doing so, they totally miss out on living. Just

for a day, stop and think about the ways you worry about keeping your body—and the bodies of your loved ones—fed, sheltered, clothed, out of harm's way, protected from break-ins or accidents, and attractive and pleasing to others. Often, we don't realize how much fear we have about simply getting out of bed in the morning because something bad might happen. This unconscious focus on death keeps joy, abundance, and a carefree feeling of wonder out of our everyday experience, robbing us of the adventures our souls came here to experience.

2. Our egos condemn us to death every day. Most of us wouldn't *think* of saying the same things to others that our egos say to ourselves. But while your ego is hypercritical, your higher Self is enjoying every moment, whether you're in a body or you're not. On a soul level, you are light energy—like a little kid, free, playful, and grateful for all the wonder in this world. When you tune in to that knowing within you, you naturally create and share your gifts. You no longer focus on what others think about you. Instead, you flow your energy freely into the world and feel alive in each moment.

3. Death does not separate you from your loved ones. If you're missing a friend or family member who has gone back Home, you may feel a longing and sadness. But their soul is every bit as alive as it ever was. In fact, you might have an even better relationship now that their ego's needs aren't in the way. Ask that person to come visit you, sit and listen, pay attention to feelings or signs that they're with you. As you tune in to this ongoing relationship, you'll find renewed joy, plus the understanding that we are eternal beings. Truly, no one ever dies.

WISDOM TEACHING 4
DIVINE LIFE

Divine Life

There is no life outside of Heaven.
—*A Course in Miracles*

When my husband and I got married, we decided to postpone our honeymoon and spend a quiet week at home, relaxing after all the wedding festivities. During that week, we went to a home improvement store to pick out a couple of items for our house.

As I stood next to my new husband, I felt such a surge of joy—what *A Course in Miracles* calls a holy instant. Right there in the plumbing aisle, I felt like I was in heaven—fully connected to divine energy, peaceful and happy, and completely alive.

At some point in your life, you may have had a moment when you were relaxing into the embrace of a loved one, moving into a cherished new home, or walking through the woods on a spring day and smelling a symphony of blossoms, and thought, "Wow. This is heaven."

It's a sumptuous moment. And it may seem like it was caused by a person, a purchase, or a place. That feeling of heaven, though, came from inside *you*. It's a state of being that you can experience no matter where you are, what you're doing, or who you're with.

In truth, it's a remembrance of the divine love that you are, a memory of the Home you carry within you always. We are always in Heaven—that's where our eternal spirits live, even when we're here in our physical bodies. When we choose to be in the energy of Heaven, we feel the power of life energy flowing through us.

1. Love and life are synonymous. We often think of love as romantic or maternal—tied to roles we play in this world. But love is the very essence of who we are. It's what we're made of. When you feel your ego fears getting hold of you, focus on love. Look at something beautiful in your surroundings. Listen to music that inspires you. Write a note of gratitude to a friend. Do something that reconnects you with love, and you will reconnect with life.
2. "Let all things be as they are." This simple but magnificent quote from the Course relieves us from the ego's constant need to judge. We have no idea how much life energy it takes to constantly evaluate ourselves and others. When we simply accept and allow, we short-circuit the ego's need to control, and we relax into our lives as they are.
3. In our natural state of Heaven, we can trust all the spiritual resources available to us. Next time your ego feels overwhelmed or angry, hand over the feelings and situation to Spirit. You were made to enjoy your life rather than worry and struggle your way through it. Say to Spirit, "I don't know how to fix this, but I know you do." Feel the relief as you release your fear and return to the love that you are.

Wisdom Teaching 5
Peace

Peace

> I could see peace instead of this.
> —*A Course in Miracles*

Peace seems to be an outward condition. We experience peace when the neighbor's dog stops barking, when politicians take a break from skewering each other, when more money comes in and you can relax about your bills for a while.

But true peace of mind is a deeper connection with Spirit, knowing that your true nature *is* peace, no matter how much chaos may go on in the world around you. As *A Course in Miracles* says, "Peace is an attribute *in* you. You cannot find it outside."

1. Every day, you can bring more peace into the world, or bring more fear. The difference is simply what you choose to focus on. Instead of, "I'm scared about the direction the world is headed," you might focus on, "I see goodness happening in my community." Instead of, "My partner is wrong and I'm right," you might shift to, "Our egos have different points of view, but his/her higher Self is love." Making deliberate choices about the thoughts you think will lead you to greater contentment and calm. This is a powerful

mantra to repeat to yourself: "I am a bringer of peace today."
2. The peace of God is your only goal. When you live from love, from your higher mind, you shift your priorities. Instead of focusing on accumulating wealth, getting a new car, or even finding a loving partner, you find peace within first. Then the outward blessings of life naturally manifest in your life.
3. Our personal contentment contributes to peace in the world. The Dalai Lama writes, "We need to encourage an understanding that inner peace comes from relying on human values like love, compassion, tolerance and honesty, and that peace in the world relies on individuals finding inner peace." Every time we choose a loving thought, we are making the world a kinder place.

WISDOM TEACHING 6
LOVE

LOVE

> I am sustained by the love of God.
> —*A Course in Miracles*

We labor under the illusion that we must make sure everything in our lives goes according to our plan, and that we must protect and defend ourselves. Meanwhile our heavenly Source is caring for us in ways that far transcend our earthly efforts. God's love for us is so profound that when realize how blessed we are, we might fall to our knees in humble gratitude.

Many years ago I was going through a rough time. My mother was in the hospital, not recovering from a surgery. My relationship with a woman I believed to be the love of my life ended. It was the depths of winter in New Jersey. As a result of hanging around the hospital visiting my mother, I contracted a staph infection that created an abscess on my lip the size of a large grape.

I went to a doctor to treat the abscess, and he lanced it without any anesthesia. I yelled so loudly that I'm sure all the people in the waiting room ran out.

Then I drove through a snowstorm to a pharmacy to get some antibiotics. As I approached the counter, everyone in line took one look at me and moved aside so I could get my medicine. Then I discovered I didn't have my wallet, and the pharmacist told me to just take the pills and forget about paying.

It felt like the worst day of my life.

When I arrived home, I opened the mailbox and found a letter from my mentor, Hilda Charlton. It was a spiritual love letter in which Hilda told me how proud she was of what I was doing, that she loved and believed in me, and she saw great things for my future. In that moment my heart found deep comfort. If there was one day in my life when I would have chosen to receive that letter, it was that day. I was a student of Hilda's for fourteen years, and that was the only time I ever received a letter from her.

A Course in Miracles asks us to remember, "By grace I live. By grace I am released." God is our loving parent who guides us impeccably and eternally. While we may go through hard times on our earthly journey, we can never sever ourselves from love, our true Source and Destiny.

1. Love knows how to find us and deliver our blessings when we need them. The universe has not abandoned us. The love that created the universe remains with us, even amid the illusions that make it seem that love is absent.
2. The voice of love works through other people and guides them to act on love's behalf. People tuned in to love are in their right place at the right time to help others. Hilda had no idea what I was going through, but her intuition had guided her perfectly.
3. No situation is ever so dire that love cannot find a way to extricate us from it. Grace supersedes karma.

Wisdom Teaching 7
True Function

True Function

> A friend is someone who sees through
> you, and still enjoys the view.
> —Wilma Askinas

Your function is what makes your life work. Fear, separation, and judgment are not a part of your function because they undermine your happiness rather than enhance it. Love, joining together, and forgiveness are your function because they bring you joy, freedom, and inner peace.

An Indian *sadhu* (holy man) discovered that a prostitute was living on his street. The sadhu stationed himself across the street from the prostitute's home and watched men enter and leave the house. For each of the prostitute's customers, the sadhu placed a stone first on the ground, then atop the pile of gathered stones. He was keeping a record of her sins.

Years later, the prostitute died, and soon afterward so did the sadhu. When the sadhu arrived at the vestibule of heaven, he looked beyond the pearly gates and saw the prostitute lounging beside a swimming pool aside a great mansion. She was eating a sumptuous meal, laughing, and enjoying the company of friends.

Soon the heavenly gatekeeper showed the sadhu to his own portion of the kingdom. The sadhu was shocked to find a small, cold stone hut. Outraged, he complained to the gatekeeper, "That woman was a prostitute, and she was given a heavenly mansion. I was a holy man, and all I get is a stone hut?"

The gatekeeper replied, "Although that woman was a prostitute, she had a good heart. She had a child she needed to support, and that was the only way she knew how to do it. She was kind to her clients and sought to heal the pain that drove them to her. You, on the other hand, spent much of your life judging her. Each judgment you laid over her was an impediment for your own soul. You have each inherited the experience equivalent to the consciousness you held in life."

1. We cannot judge what other people are doing. When we slip into the consciousness of judgment, we only hurt ourselves. Our purpose in life is to see the best in others, even amid their human frailties. We never know why another person is doing something, or how their acts fit into the greater picture of their spiritual evolution and how they affect the world.
2. Our worldly occupation is meaningful only if it aligns with our spiritual purpose. Some people may have a religious or holy vocation, but it is what is going on inside their soul that determines whether their path is holy or not. Any path can be divine if we bring a higher consciousness to it.
3. The purpose of all relationships is to empower others and ourselves to be all we can be. We must constantly choose to validate the highest version of them and

ourselves. Only the attributes of God befit us. When we see others as God sees them, we are on course with our purpose in the world, and we affirm their roles in the divine plan.

Wisdom Teaching 8
Destiny

Destiny

> Now you are among the saviors of the world.
> Your destiny lies there and nowhere else.
> —*A Course in Miracles*

This quote from *ACIM* may seem intimidating at first. Savior of the world? We're taught that's Jesus's job, or the work of other divine masters. But we're all here to save ourselves and each other from thinking we're separate and alone. That's what our relationships are for. Truly, our destiny is to be good to one another. To be kind and compassionate. To be forgiving.

Our egos think our destiny is a perfect love, a perfect job, a perfect success. But our true destiny is to remember that we are Spirit, and everything we create in our lives will be a reflection of that truth.

1. Destiny is not a predetermined script for your life. Destiny means leaning into your true self more and more each day until love, not fear, becomes your current moment and your trajectory. Deep within you is a memory of who and what you were created to be. As you sit in silence and listen to your heart, you can remember your true function, the gifts and talents within, the desires that call you forward, the dreams

that have always stirred within your soul. Remember, destiny isn't always about *what* you do. It's about the feelings of inner peace that enliven *all* that you do.
2. Destiny reveals itself to you moment by moment. In every conversation, every relationship, every thought, lies the potential for feeling connected to your Self, Spirit, and those around you. This destiny—to remember and remind others that we are not separate and alone—will bring you the greatest peace and contentment because you'll be fulfilling your destiny as an expression of love and unity. Even when your ego disagrees with others or goes into judgment mode, your higher Self will remember that Oneness is at your core.
3. Your destiny is to see the light in everyone. Impossible? To the ego, definitely. But looking through the lens of the higher Self is like seeing others the way Spirit does. You look beyond the fear, the personality, the body—all the symbols of separation. And instead, you see the soul, loving and peaceful, just like you.

WISDOM TEACHING 9
DIVINE DOING

Divine Doing

> What would You have me do?
> Where would You have me go?
> What would You have me say, and to whom?
> —*A Course in Miracles*

We're made for action. Our ears, eyes, mouths, hands, and feet allow us to create new experiences, communicate with others, and bring new thoughts into being.

Often, though, we get overwhelmed and exhausted by to-do lists or other people's expectations of what we "should" be doing. This is because our egos are trying hard to achieve and overcome their feelings of self-doubt and low self-worth.

Our doing, though, can be inspired by love rather than driven by fear. When we tune in to Source, listen for guidance, and act on that inner wisdom, the hard work of everyday life starts to dissolve into a more effortless, satisfying, and effective flow.

And what if you don't know *what* to do? If you simply can't decide? Move into your higher Mind, connect with Source, and ask yourself, "What would love do now?" Listen for a moment. Love will have an answer.

1. Focus on intention first, action second. For instance, if you're trying to meet a deadline at work, take a few deep breaths, close your eyes, and connect with your *why*. "I get satisfaction from completing my work on time and well. I love going home at the end of the day knowing I did my part. I care about moving this project forward because I can see how it'll help our customers." This is very different from the ego's story: "I'm tired and I just want this job to be done." Action based on the ego will feel like you're pushing a boulder uphill. Action based on loving intention will feel like skipping stones down a country road.
2. Divine doers do only what they truly enjoy. Your ego will jump up and fly the Selfish flag at the thought of this, but your higher mind knows that you serve others best when you do what you love. *Doing* to please others engages the ego's belief in sacrifice and struggle, which leads to resentment. Instead of bringing more resentment into the world, bring in more love and joy. Try doing something in a new way—even if it's experimenting with a new recipe or taking a different route home from the supermarket. Do what you feel inspired to do in the moment, and give yourself permission to be delighted.
3. Your imagination loves to envision exciting new actions. As a divine doer, you create your own dreams and aspirations from a place of playfulness and wonder. Wake up in the morning, and before you get out of bed, say to your Self and Spirit, "I love the ease and flow of my life. I can't wait to create some joy today."

Wisdom Teaching 10
Divine Being

DIVINE BEING

> A miracle is never lost. It may touch many
> people you have not even met, and produce
> undreamed of changes in situations of
> which you are not even aware.
> —*A Course in Miracles*

Because we are spiritual beings, it is the nature of our spirit, or heart, that determines the quality of life and our effect on others. We tend to measure our success by actions and material results, but real success is a quality of experience. To know yourself as a radiant soul is to know yourself as God knows you.

Rushing through the San Francisco airport on my way to catch a flight, I felt harried and anxious. As I looked around, it seemed that the people around me were likewise preoccupied and distraught.

Then I saw a fellow approaching me who looked different from the others. In contrast to the frenzy most passengers displayed, this man's face exuded utter peace. His physical appearance was quite normal. He was dressed in common garb, not the robe of a priest or any holy vocation. Yet his energy was immensely soothing, his face soft, eyes clear, and his body fluid. The moment I saw him, I relaxed. My shoulders dropped, my solar plexus unclenched, and my pace slowed. In his presence I experienced a profound healing.

I do not know who that man was, and I never saw him again. Perhaps he was an angel. Or simply a soul at peace. That encounter occurred many years ago, but to this day I count him as one of my most significant teachers of peace. I still talk and write about him. Though he knows it not, he changed my life.

1. We can call ourselves successful only when our soul is at peace. It does not matter so much what we are doing. *Who we are* while we are doing it and *how we are doing it* determines the value of the experience. We are human *beings* more than human doings. We may be doing all the right things, or properly going through the motions of life, but unless we are quiet inside, we are not accomplishing what we came to do.
2. No external situation, such as a busy airport, is necessarily a cause for stress. All stress is attitudinal. We can shift our attitude at any moment and move from stress to peace, from fear to love.
3. When you are at one with your divine being, you exert a profound impact on the people and world about you, such that you can heal them with your energy. You may exert an influence on their life that you never know about. Meanwhile, you have sent out ripples of well-being that uplift the universe.

There is only one science, love, one riches, love, only one policy, love.
To make love is all the law and the prophets.
—Anatole France

Wisdom Teaching 11
Divine Evolution

Divine Evolution

> God is but love, and therefore so am I.
> —*A Course in Miracles*

The Self we present to the world is always a representation of the inner mind. No matter what the situation, we're always doing one of two things: projecting fear from the ego mind or extending love from our higher mind.

As we evolve, we have the chance to grow and expand our consciousness in every moment by choosing what *A Course in Miracles* calls "right-mindedness." This means being in harmony with the Divine love that created us by tuning to the love within.

When you do this, you realize these things...

1. Everything you experience is an opportunity to love yourself more. This may seem selfish; aren't we supposed to love others first? But when we truly, deeply love the joy and peace within us, we naturally share it with the world. Instead of beating ourselves up when we think we've made a mistake, we can feel the love within and be gentle with ourselves, which allows us to be compassionate and forgiving with others.
2. We're all here to support one another. To the ego, relationships are about *getting* from a consciousness

of scarcity. To the higher mind, they're about *giving* from a consciousness of abundance. You were created with natural gifts, and when you give those away to others, you have more of them, not less. When you share who you truly are rather than trying to please others, you grow, and so do those around you.

3. You can't *not* be the child of Divine love that you are. Spirit is your DNA. The world of the ego teaches that you're broken or sinful, but the opposite is true. You are whole and blessed—the grace of God made manifest. It's only when we listen to the fear-based voices of the world, and of our own egos, that we forget who and what we truly are. By spending more time each day asking for and tuning in to guidance from the Divine, you start to move away from ego judgments and grievances. This is your evolution—from fear-based ego to Divine love.

Wisdom Teaching 12
Divine Involution

Divine Involution

> You are the light of the world.
> —*A Course in Miracles*

One of the hardest things you may ever do is look in the mirror and say, "I matter."

Our egos tell us we're not enough and catalog every "mistake" we make. Plus, the voices of everyone who ever criticized or hurt us echo within that ego mind. If we're looking for evidence that we're screwing up our lives, we don't have to look far to find it.

But that simply means we're listening to the wrong voice within us.

When you live from your inner Self, you realize that Heaven is a state of being right now. You're not here to prove your worth, earn the grace of God, or struggle and sacrifice your way to success. You are here as an expression of Divine love, and you can choose the thoughts that come from that in every moment by listening to the love within.

1. The inner voice is quiet because there is no conflict in it. On a typical day, we're all bombarded by the noisy, demanding, angry, insistent voices of fear. This can make it hard to hear the quiet inner voice of your true Self and of Spirit. Those voices speak

from peace and contentment, which makes them naturally quiet, easily drowned out. That's why it's so important to have a spiritual practice of meditation, journaling, or walking—whatever quiets you enough to hear beyond the fear.
2. We don't know anything about anything. Eager as our egos might be to come up with a plan, fix the world (or our spouse!), or prove themselves right, we don't know enough to judge. Think about all the "problems" you've fretted about in the past that somehow worked out without your hard work or worry. That's because our guides and angels, in concert with our higher minds, are orchestrating events with divine order. Everything truly works out for us when we let it.
3. See the love of God everywhere. It *is* everywhere. The "trick" is to focus not on what you're looking at, but what lens you're looking through. When you consistently see through the eyes of love, you see love everywhere you look because that's what you are. As a friend said, "I send everyone love, because that's all I've got."

Wisdom Teaching 13
Unification

UNIFICATION

All of the problems and sorrows of the world issue from the fictitious belief that we are bodies only, separate from each other and God. The key to healing is to remember that there is one God Who expresses through each and all of us.

Ramana Maharshi was a great Indian saint who experienced sudden enlightenment at age sixteen, which sustained for the rest of his life. He realized his true self to be God and encouraged us to do the same. His singular teaching was to constantly inquire, "Who am I?"

When Robert Adams visited the sage's ashram, Sri Ramana welcomed him, treated him as an honored guest, and brought food to his room. The master took care of his disciples as if *they* were the saints. When Ramana Maharshi was on his deathbed, a pet peacock sat on the roof, screeching. The master's last words were, "Has anyone fed the peacock yet?"

Enlightenment does not imply escape from the world; to the contrary, it implies mastery of it. Spiritual masters do not set themselves off from humanity but heal the world from within it. Jesus washed his disciples' feet, teaching, "He who humbles himself shall be exalted."

Avatar Meher Baba traveled around India and cared for God-intoxicants, people attached to the world by the thinnest of threads. In our society, such people would be considered mentally ill or catatonic. Yet the spiritual tradition of India reframes these souls as absorbed in the divine. Meher Baba journeyed to tiny, remote villages, bowed to these people, and washed their feet. His motto was "mastery through servitude."

In Western culture we tend to put spiritually advanced people on pedestals and pamper them. Meanwhile, they are thinking about how to unite with their students. Ramana Maharshi slept in the same house with his disciples, shared meals, took daily walks with them, and did not set himself apart from humanity. His attitude was, "We're all in this together."

1. The ego creates hierarchies of holiness and sets certain individuals up as closer to God, while others are lesser. This is a dangerous ploy that denies equal divinity in all. Consider whom you believe is closer to God than you are, and imagine that you are equal to that person in Spirit. Knowing your oneness, how would you interact with that person differently?
2. *A Course in Miracles* asks us to remember, "When I am healed, I am not healed alone." Because there is only one mind, when you awaken, you stimulate others to awaken. Your healing is your gift to humanity.

Should you be tempted to define another person by your differences with them, notice how it feels to be separate. Then shift your vision to pierce beyond appearances and recognize the glory and wholeness of their spirit. Notice what happens in your mental, emotional, and physical experience when you drop into a peaceful sense of spiritual sameness.

About the Authors

Since 2007, **Adam C. Hall** has been conserving land and working with global evolutionary leaders as the founder of the EarthKeeper Alliance. Adam's teachings integrate science, spirituality and success. A trained shaman and teacher of *A Course in Miracles*, he is the creator of the Genius Process and the founder/CEO at the Genius Studio. Adam has four decades of experience as an impact investor and entrepreneur.

Adam has been a guest on over one hundred radio/TV shows and more than forty talks and keynotes. He is is a three-time published author and has been a featured presenter at numerous summits. He is a proud father of three daughters, has seven granddaughters, and lives in Santa Barbara.

Please visit his web site at AdamCHall.com

"Adam C. Hall's book, *Divine Genius*, is a consciousness template to apply Quantum Physics in real life. He helps the reader rise above disempowering programs to manifest our intentions and thrive into the future. I highly recommend it as a guide to free ourselves by freeing our minds."

—Bruce H. Lipton, PhD, epigenetic science pioneer, and bestselling author of *The Biology of Belief*

Alan Cohen, MA, is the author of thirty popular inspirational books, including the best-selling *A Course in Miracles Made Easy* and *The Dragon Doesn't Live Here Anymore*, the award-winning *A Deep Breath of Life*, and the classic *Are You as Happy as Your Dog?*

His books have been translated into twenty-five foreign languages. His work has been featured on Oprah.com and in *USA Today*, *The Washington Post*, and *101 Top Experts*. Alan's radio program *Get Real* has been broadcast weekly on Hay House Radio, and his monthly column *From the Heart* is featured in magazines internationally.

Alan is a respected keynoter and seminar leader for professional meetings in the fields of personal growth, inspiration, holistic health, human relations, and achievement of work/life balance. He has served as instructor of Individual and Group Dynamics at Montclair State College, stood on the faculty of Omega Institute for Holistic Studies, and is a professor at EnTheos Academy for Optimal Living. He is a featured presenter in the award-winning documentary *Finding Joe*, which celebrates the teachings of visionary mythologist Joseph Campbell.

Alan brings a warm blend of wisdom, intimacy, humor, and vision to the path of personal, professional, and spiritual growth. He loves to extract lessons from the practical experiences of daily living and find beauty in the seemingly mundane.

You can reach him at alancohen.com.

Debra Landwehr Engle is the author of four books of nonfiction, including *The Only Little Prayer You Need: The Shortest Route to a Life of Joy, Abundance and Peace of Mind*, which was translated into four languages and has been an international bestseller. It features a foreword by His Holiness the Dalai Lama and an endorsement by Archbishop Emeritus Desmond Tutu. She is a two-time winner of the Nautilus Award, honoring better books for a better world.

A longtime teacher of *A Course in Miracles,* Debra has offered workshops and classes worldwide based on her books and the principles of *ACIM.*

She has worked in publishing her entire career, beginning as a newspaper copywriter and *Better Homes and Gardens* book editor, then starting a thriving freelance business. She's written and edited hundreds of articles for such national publications as *Better Homes and Gardens, Country Home, Country Gardens,* and other lifestyle magazines.

Debra holds an MFA in creative nonfiction from Goucher College in Baltimore. Now managing director of the international Story Summit, she works with budding authors one-on-one, in small groups, and through retreats and online courses.

You can reach her at debraengle.com.

www.ingramcontent.com/pod-product-compliance
Lightning Source LLC
Chambersburg PA
CBHW070655050426
42451CB00008B/365